The man. His surroundings and his childhood

A white-haired man with deep blue eyes and a beard is crossing a street near the Church of the Sagrada Familia; he is very simply dressed and looks somewhat preoccupied and a bit annoyed. He has just had another discussion with one of the craftsmen working on the church and as always, the amount of work he has on his hands has made him late again. He never carries a watch and when he is preoccupied, he completely forgets about the time; for him there is no set meal-time or bed-time.

This man who devoted himself so whole heartedly to his work was Antoni Gaudí. He was born in Reus on June 25, 1852. His father was a coppersmith in the nearby village of Riudoms. He was the youngest of five children and although he left Reus at an early age to go to live in Barcelona, he always kept a strong attachment to the country as well as his quick temper. Shortly before his death, he still remarked, «I've managed to master nearly everything except my bad temper.»

His strong personality stood out already when he was a young boy. At school he was noted for his resolute character which led him to apply himself diligently to the things he was interested in and totally ignore those that did not appeal to him. This, of course, made his marks very inconsistant and greatly puzzled both his teachers and his parents who never quite knew where that strong-willed boy was heading.

Already in his youth, he applied himself with the same tenacity to whatever he had on his hands as did this old man crossing the street without looking, and who we are going to tell you a few things about in hopes that it will help you get to know him and his work a little better.

Animals and nature

Young Antoni loved to go hiking. While he was out in the country and in the mountains, he would take note of everything he saw because he was always eager to learn any lesson nature might have in store for him.

Later, his long walks in the country and his keen sense of observation made him realize that nature was offering him solutions to the problems he was encountering in his buildings. And so he began to apply to architecture the lessons he had learned from everyday life.

He converted many of the living creatures around him into elements of decoration. In this respect, if you look closely, you will find insects for door-knockers, tortoises supporting columns, leaves joined together as doorways, climbing vines on the walls of rooms, clambering dragons looking at you from the most unexpected places, etc.

He did not, however, use these lessons from nature only as decorations, he also made good use of the things he had learned on his hikes to give greater stability to his buildings.

In order to fully appreciate his keen sense of observation, look closely at the animals, or better yet the plants he used in decorating his buildings, and you will even be able to recognize different species; that is how faithful his reproductions are.

In this respect, we can assure you that he learned more from a few odd jobs that he took on while still at school than from all the academic instruction he received.

Since his father was not what you would call rich, Antoni had to work his way through school which meant, head-strong as he was, he was constantly looking for little jobs with different architects. The kind of work that required immediate solutions to practical problems interested him more than all the theoretical problems proposed at school.

After he graduated, he began receiving commissions from people. He carried out these little jobs with the same enthusiasm as he would later on his great works.

To fully appreciate what we are saying, take a look at the lamp posts in the Plaza Real in Barcelona and you will see that they are made with the greatest of care. Well, they belong to the time when Gaudí was still a young architect.

Schooling and early works

In 1873, with his mind made up and with a real desire to study, he enrolled at the School of Architecture in Barcelona.

His enthusiasm for the school soon waned and, notwithstanding the great works he was to produce later, he did not apply himself very much. It was easy to see that this young student from Reus had no taste for academic discipline; something deep inside him made him pay more attention to his own impulses than to the perscribed norms, to direct experience rather than to book-learning, to his own personal taste rather than to the established rules.

Two characteristics of his work: imagination and craftsmanship

As you become acquainted with Gaudí's work you will realize that his buildings differ from those of other architects in that they look as if they were the fruit of pure imagination. You forget that they are houses made of stone, iron, wood and other unromantic materials.

True enough, but if your gaze lingers on each of the elements of which these buildings are composed, you will see that this was only possible because the architect was thoroughly familiar with all the materials and it was precisely this knowledge that made it possible for him to carry out the dictates of his imagination.

He fantasized, but he also knew how to turn his fancies into reality. He could do so because he was one of the few architects thoroughly familiar with the skills of other crafts. Because he was a sculptor, a blacksmith, a carpenter and other things at the same time, he could explain to the men working for him just how he wanted that tortoise destined to support a column, or that palm tree shaped archway or that mosaic made from broken bits of ceramic tile which was to decorate some whimsical construction he was busy with.

These crafts, which he had learned as a student, remained with him throughout his entire lifetime. Working with his hands was for him a form of daily exercise that brought him in close contact with the materials and allowed him to get to know all their secrets.

He kept this up even into old age; in fact, when he died it was discovered that at the time he had been working on some bronze lamps which he was fashioning with his own hands.

BARCELO...
Le vieux
maître t...
vaille en...
core en...
MULTIPL...
PROJECTS...
DE DECO...
TIÓN ET...
à l'inve...
tión de...
bibelo...
qui so...
un pe...
morce...
de sa...

Houses in Barcelona

Gaudí's works can be found in various places, some as far away as Astorga, León, Santander or Majorca, but we will limit ourselves to those he built in Barcelona because in just this small area we can find enough important buildings to understand how his work developed.

Since we would like you to go yourselves to each of these houses, playing the role of a detective trying to identify the elements this gifted architect used in his constructions, we will only give you a few clues to facilitate the task.

Casa Vicens (The Vicens House)

This was the summer residence of a tile merchant; it was Gaudí's first important commission. That may have been the reason why he put all his wits together to come up with a house that looked like an outburst of imagination.

The Rainbow Fountain, where the water flows over the metal bars and breaks up into the colours of the rainbow as the sunlight hits it, is a clear example of this. Inside the house, there is a room where the ceiling is covered with cherries and the walls are full of birds and flamingoes, creating a fairy tale atmosphere. Look carefully and you will see on the walls different inscriptions like «Sol, solet» (Sunshine, my little sunshine) or «Oh, l'ombra de l'estiu» (Oh, the shade of summer) and others that you are likely to discover.

Colegio de las Teresianas (The Teresian Nuns' School)

The budget for this building, which was to house a school run by the Teresian nuns, was rather limited so Gaudí produced a more sober project than on other occasions.

We mention this to emphasis the fact that on this occasion he concentrated especially on integrating large areas and skillfully distributing the light, particularly in the corridors. Needless to say, he was highly successfully in achieving both.

Casa Calvet (The Calvet House)

This was the first apartment building Gaudí worked on; he received this commission from a textile merchant.

Taking into account the fact that the merchant was particularly fond of mushrooms, the architect used various types of mushrooms and toadstools in the decoration of the handrails and the stone reliefs.

Gaudí involved himself so completely in the construction of his buildings that for this house he even designed the furniture.

By way of curiosity, we would like to draw your attention to the bug-shaped doorknocker.

Bellesguard (The Bellesguard House)

In 1900, Gaudí was commissioned to build a house on the very site where King Martin the Human (1395-1410) had built himself a small retreat outside the city. The architect was able to respect the ruins and successfully incorporate them into the construction.

If you look at the Bellesguard House from a distance, you will see that the building and the mountain blend in, forming a magical composition thanks to the architect's brilliant idea of making the walls of the house the same colour as the mountain.

As you contine in your search for curious details, notice the door knockers; this time they take the shape of human bones.

Casa Batlló (The Batllo House)

Some textile manufacturers commissioned Gaudí to restore the façade of their house in Passeig de Gràcia; here the architect gave free rein to his imagination. The slanted roof over the garrets became the back of a dragon; the columns were covered with vegetable motifs and floral reliefs; the chimneys were transformed into fanciful shapes full of colour; the facade of the house was covered with bits of ceramic and crystal; even the furniture took on the shape of human bones.

It was as if a fairy had come to Passeig de Gràcia and had changed the house into something right out of a fairy tale.

CASA BATLLÓ

Casa Milà (The Mila House)

As you approach the Mila House you have the impression that a huge rocky cliff had suddenly sprung up in the midst of the houses and buildings. No, it is not an urban mountain, but the last house Gaudí built before shutting himself away to work exclusively on the Sagrada Familia.

An army of chimneys and air shafts watches over the house from the terrace, as if they were sentinels mimicking the billowy smoke rising to the sky.

Another innovation Gaudí tried in this house was an interior ramp making it possible for the carriages to deposit their occupants at the very doors of their apartments. One could hardly ask for greater luxury!

The Güells

Certain people played a key role in Gaudí's life; they made it possible for him to achieve several of his major works. They were the Güells and the Comilla family.

The Güell family was one of the wealthiest at that time and when they met Gaudí, they confided so entirely in his ability that they gave him all the freedom and the means his inspiration required.

Eusebi Güell, especially, cherished the same creative ideals as Gaudí and because of that they got along very well from the start.

Pabellones Güell (The Güell Pavilions)

Among other things, the Güell family commissioned Gaudí to do the entrance pavilions (the gatehouse and the stables) and the main gate to their property on the outskirts of the city, where today the Palace of Pedralbes stands.

The main gate, which can be seen from the street, is a magnificent winged dragon which, we can say without fear of exaggerating, is the most outstanding of all the different representations of the dragon used by Gaudí. We must point out that the shape of the dragon's body follows the position of the stars in the Constellations of Draco and of Hercules.

Palacio Güell (The Güell Palace)

Two years later he was commissioned to build the family's residence in Barcelona.

On this occasion, he used his imagination to the utmost as can be seen throughout the entire building, from the basement to the chimneys; it all reminds us of a fairy tale forest.

Everything in this palace is surprising and fanciful, from the suspended staircases to the ventilation system or the great organ or the closet-like chapel or the forty some different types of columns found throughout.

Cripta Güell (The Güell Crypt)

At Santa Coloma de Cervelló, Count Güell built a textile factory with housing facilities for the workers. Gaudí made the crypt for what was to have been the church.

This is the most incomplete piece of all of Gaudí's works. Nevertheless, it is, without a doubt, the most perfect as far as construction is concerned and the most original and daring of all his achievements.

In order to understand the difficulties he encountered while working on it, note that the draft was drawn up in 1898, the project begun in 1908 and the work interrupted in 1917.

One detail of the construction will give you a better understanding of the way Gaudí worked: on the site where the steps up to the church were to be, there stood a hundredyear-old pine tree. The thought of having to cut it down appalled him so that he preferred to alter the entire flight of steps rather than cut down a tree that had stood there for so many years.

Güell Park

One of Count Güell's most cherished dreams was to build a large garden-city where the houses and nature blended in together in an area where over fifty per cent was gardens, trees and space for children to play and adults to stroll, read or simply relax.

He gave the job to his friend Gaudí who undertook it with great pleasure because he loved the idea. In spite of their enthusiasm, the construction of the park was unfortunately interrupted by the war and finally stopped altogether with the death of the Count.

of steps with a curious likeness of a reptile; something between a nice friendly dragon and some sort of lizard.

The big square meant for open-air concerts or plays or festivals and which today is actually serving its original purpose was also completed.

As you walk up the winding paths on the hillside where this little town was to have been, it is easy to imagine the beauty of the entire setting with its sixty houses by just looking at the three that were built: one for the Güells, now a school; another for a lawyer whose family still lives there; and another for Gaudí himself, now turned into a museum.

What was built, however, was the entrance with its iron gate in the shape of a kind of palm leave very characteristic of Catalonia —the country Gaudí loved so deeply and always defended— and a flight

This square is supported by eighty-six columns which at the same time were to be the setting for the open market-place. The square is bordered by a bench that stretches itself almost all the way round in undulating waves. The whole thing is a huge jigsaw puzzle made of thousands of tiny pieces of ceramic tile, glassware, crockery, etc. Whenever you visit the park try to find out what the pieces are made of and what they were part of and you will see how much fun it is.

Inside the houses

Perhaps because he looked so often to nature, Antoni Gaudí understood that all things are inter-related, there are no isolated elements and everything is related to its surroundings.

This variety, which is present all aspects of our lives and our environment, can clearly be applied to architecture.

That is why he understood a house as a whole, and did not spend his time contemplat-

ing how to solve one or another of the problems which emerged during the construction of the building. Only when the construction was complete did he work untiringly to apply his inspired solutions to every aspect.

For that reason, in the interiors of his houses it is possible to find, for example, an imitation of countryside forms such as the dunes which appear in the ceiling plaster of the Casa Milà. We can see how he experiments with the use of new materials for existing forms, such as the sack-like forms of the iron balconies in the Casa Milà.

CASA
MILÀ

CASA BATLLÓ

CASA VICENS

CASA BATLLÓ

Another passionate theme for Gaudí was his use of light. A clear example of this is found in the Casa Vicens, where the walls of the dining room, the smoking room and the gallery are decorated with Chinese figures and numerous paintings, which could be seen as creatinga closed atmosphere, but which Gaudí overcomes using light which enters from the gallery.

In the Casa Milà there are countless decorative elements, from the ceiling inscriptions, such as «sota l'ombreta, l'ombrí, flors i violes i romaní» (extract from a traditional song - In the shade, flowers, violets and rosemary), to the doorknobs and handles, and the tortoise-shaped glass pieces.

But his interest in ALL the elements contained in a home is best seen in the Casa Batlló; everything, from the staircases to the ceilings, the fireplaces and the dining room furniture, shows an array of solutions conceived and employed in order to create a unique setting.

La Sagrada Familia
(The Church of the Sacred Family)

Gaudí was a profoundly religious man. So when he heard that the Sagrada Familia was to be the cathedral of the new Barcelona, he was so enthusiastic about it that although the work had already been begun by another architect, he readily took it over and began introducing changes.

As time passed (remember that he started working on the church already in 1884), he became more and more engrossed in the project. In fact, so great was the attraction he felt for it that after 1908 he dedicated himself entirely to the construction of the Sagrada Familia and refused to take on any other jobs.

The design he had in mind was fantastic: eighteen towers were to surround the naves making it look like a true apotheosis of pinacles and towers which, by the way, were to resemble the human towers the Xiquets from Valls erect. In addition, the church was to be accompanied by schools, residences, meeting halls, etc.

Of all the work that was put into it, Gaudí was only able to see completed the crypt, the apse and the Nativity Façade which is like an enormous nativity scene so important in itself that it could be considered a building in its own right. In fact, for many years it has been one of the best known symbols of Barcelona.

Gaudí wanted this temple to be the sum-total of all his research and discoveries and now that you know his work a little better, you can just imagine what that meant.

On the Nativity Façade alone, there are more than thirty different species of plants corresponding to thirty varieties cultivated in the Holy Land. Plants, animals and geometric figures cover the entire construction; each with its own symbolism. Here is an example: there are two columns resting on two splendid stone tortoises; if you look carefully, you will see that the one on the seaward side is a marine turtle while the one on the other side is an ordinary tortoise like one you might have in your own back yard.

PROJECTE
TEMPLE
SAGRADA
FAMÍLIA

Gaudí
ARQ.

FAÇANA DE
LA GLÒRIA

Antoni Gaudí died on the 10th of June, 1926. Upon leaving his work on the Sagrada Familia, he stepped out into the street without looking and was knocked down by a tram.

Seriously injured, he was taken to the public hospital but because of his shabby clothes, no one recognized him there. When they eventually found out who he was, his friends suggested he be moved to a private clinic but he refused, saying: «My place is here amongst the poor.»

The mark of Gaudí

It has already been mentioned that Gaudí created works in other cities. For example, the Vil·la El Capricho in Comillas, Santander, where the Marquis of Comillas spent his summers. The Episcopal Palace in Astorga (León) was built in a very different style to the more usual 'gothic' works. Gaudí also participated in the restoration of Palma cathedral in Majorca.

All of this shows how Gaudí's works extend from his initial projects, such as his collaboration with Josep Fontserè in making the monuments of the Ciutadella Park, to his final smaller works in churches in Blanes and Valencia.

But official recognition aside, the work of Antoni Gaudí will never cease to impress, and from it we can learn to take a different look at nature, and understand that everything that surrounds us, even the smallest details, have a place and an importance that must be taken into account.

LEÓN · CASA DE LOS BOTINES